All original artwork created by Jed Bruce
For My Daughter, Neekka

The Story of Joe Journeyman was written and created by David Bazzoni
For Mom, Dad, Whitney, Steve & Everyone at IDNA Brands

Joe Journeyman Volume 1 Creative Team

Jed Bruce, David & Whitney Bazzoni, Eric Stendahl, Kaitlyn Murphy, Ryan Nord, Joey Hickerson, Mark Jablonski, Josh Ogden

Printed in China
Published by IDNA Brands
ISBN: 978-0-9906308-0-7
LCCN: 2015940810

2015 NFL Properties LLC

WWW.JOEJOURNEYMAN.COM
WWW.IDNABRANDS.COM

his is the story of Joe Journeyman – the only player to play for all thirty-two teams in the National Football League. No one has ever done this before Joe, and most people say no one will ever do it again.

Thankfully for Joe, he travels in style from city to city in the super cool JourneyVan. Along for the ride, every step of the way, are Joe's best friends and supporters: End Zone Ernie the Elephant, Super Fan Franny the Fox, Pom Pom Polly, the one and only Touchdown Ted the Turtle, and yours truly – ME – Leon the Lion.

As you can see within these pages, we experience some *wild* and *wacky* things along the way. Trying to keep track of each other is a full-time job. Joe, in particular, has the hardest time keeping track of his playbook. To make matters worse, a very jealous kitty cat named *Copy Cat Carl* is always lurking in the shadows, waiting for that perfect moment to steal Joe's playbook and put an end to our incredible journey. Without our playbook, Joe will be defeated and we can't move onto the next city.

That's why we need your help! As a team, it's our job to stop *Copy Cat Carl* and find Joe's playbook before that mischievous kitty cat can get his furry little paws on our secret plays.

So, what are we waiting for!? It's time to search!

Leon The Lion

TOUCHDOWN TED !

Touchdown Ted is the life of the party. He's outgoing, fun loving, and supremely confident in his own shell. Ted looks up to Joe Journeyman more than anyone in the world, but deep down in his turtle heart, Ted knows that he's a big star, too. Whenever Joe is feeling down, he can rely on Ted's bigger than life personality to cheer him up!

TED

POM POM POLLY

Pom Pom Polly is the team's cheerleader. In college, Polly was an All-American gymnast, so she knows a thing or two about tumbling. With her amazing flips Polly has a knack for getting the crowd pumped up before the big game. Polly also knows thousands of cheers by heart and *always* knows the perfect moment for the perfect cheer. GO-JOE-GO!

POLLY

LEON THE LION

Leon the Lion is Joe's best friend and trainer. He is the wise and mature one of the group, always keeping the gang out of trouble. Leon is also a football genius. Over the years, Leon has compiled a playbook full of amazing plays that are nearly impossible to defend. He also mentors Joe in tough times and encourages Joe to always do the right thing and to always treat others with respect.

LEON

END ZONE ERNIE

End Zone Ernie is the team driver. He drives the JourneyVan from stadium to stadium all across the country. He likes to drive with his trunk because it's easier on his back during those long road trips. Ernie is also the team researcher. Ernie loves to read all about each new city and then share everything he's learned with the team. Ernie especially likes to learn about (and then eat) the local food! Yum!

SUPER FAN FRANNY

Super Fan Franny is the team's personal trainer. Let's just say that she has her hands full with Ernie and Ted, who aren't always thrilled to get up and work out. When Joe and Leon are off practicing, Franny is dragging Ted and Ernie out of the JourneyVan and into the gym. Franny believes that daily exercise is very important in order for the gang to finish their journey. On game day, Franny can usually be found interacting with Joe's fans and encouraging them to be active.

COPYCAT CARL

Copy Cat Carl is Joe Journeyman's arch nemesis. His #1 goal is to steal Joe Journeyman's missing playbook and make copies of Leon's secret plays. Carl is a skilled knitter and can entrap you with his ball of yarn in a matter of seconds. He is also armed with a bottle of milk that energizes his mischievous ways. Copy Cat Carl would love nothing more than to see Joe fail, and the journey end for everyone!

BALTIMORE
RAVENS

BALTIMORE — As the members of the Baltimore Marching Ravens spelled out the name "J-O-E" the crowd erupted with enthusiasm as the real life Joe Journeyman got ready to play in his first game with his new team.

The inner harbor was rocking, the stands were festive, and the sky was beautifully mysterious as the Ravens shocked the Pittsburgh Steelers in triple overtime.

Although no pictures were taken, fans from all over the stadium claimed to see hundreds- if not thousands- of ravens flying through the sky and then forming the team's logo high above the water.

On such a wild and wacky night in Baltimore, just about anything seems possible...

PACKERS

GREEN BAY- Joe Journeyman and the Green Bay Packers defeated the Chicago Bears on an ice-cold afternoon. Despite blizzard-like conditions, superstar Joe Journeyman made an incredible last second catch in the corner of the end zone to propel the PACK to a one point victory over the Bears. Following Journeyman's miraculous one-handed reception, PACKERS fans welcomed a snow-covered Journeyman as he leaped into the stands to celebrate.

REDSKINS

LANDOVER — What a *monument*-al performance by Joe Journeyman last night in our nation's capital! Fans from all over Washington were chanting "M-V-P" as Journeyman led his teammates off the field in victory. After Joe's unbelievable five touchdown, six sack, and two interception performance, Joe left us all wondering, "what could possibly be next?!"

JOE-4-President?

LIONS

DETROIT— It's Thanksgiving in America and that means football in DETROIT!

Adding another chapter to one of the NFL's greatest traditions, dating all the way back to 1934, Joe Journeyman and the Detroit Lions are ready to kickoff against their Turkey Day rival, the Green Bay Packers. The entire Pride of Detroit has come together to ROAR-fully cheer on their beloved team on a beautiful November night in the Motor City.

Gobble, Gobble football fans!

JETS

EAST RUTHERFORD — J-E-T-S, Jets! Jets! Jets! The New York Jets were simply unstoppable on Sunday night with Joe Journeyman leading the way at quarterback. As the final seconds ticked off the clock, a boisterous chant could be heard throughout "The Big Apple" in honor of their new star.

J-O-E, GO! JOE! GO!

EAGLES

PHILADELPHIA – E-A-G-L-E-S, Eagles!

The Eagles dished out a heavy dose of tough love in a 33-3 victory over the Dallas Cowboys. The atmosphere outside of the stadium was EGGciting, to say the least, as fans soared in from all over the country to witness superstar Joe Journeyman play in his first game. From the opening flip of the coin, it was clear that the team in green and white would emerge victorious.

After all, "We got Joe, don't ya know!?"

GIANTS

EAST RUTHERFORD — Welcome Joe Journeyman to the "Big Apple!" Earlier today, fans from all over the world got their first chance to see Joe (and his buddies) on the marvelous billboards throughout Times Square in N.Y.C. Ernie, Polly, Ted, Franny, Leon, and even *Copy Cat Carl* will be chanting "GO BIG BLUE" as Joe leads the New York Football Giants onto the field.

COWBOYS

ARLINGTON, TX — How 'Bout Them Cowboys!

They say everything is bigger in Texas. With the addition of superstar Joe Journeyman, things just got even bigger for the Dallas Cowboys. In his first game with 'America's Team', against a beautiful Texas-sized sunset, Journeyman and the Cowboys defeated the Philadelphia Eagles 48-42. With time expiring, Journeyman carried a host of Eagles into the end zone to lift the Cowboys to a thrilling double overtime victory.

As the referee thrust his hands into the air to signal the game-winning touchdown, Journeyman flashed a big ol' Texas-sized smile to a very happy Lone Star state.

Steelers

PITTSBURGH—In a game full of fireworks, the Pittsburgh Steelers saved their grand finale for the perfect moment in last evening's victory over the Baltimore Ravens. With only 0:04 remaining in regulation, Joe Journeyman intercepted the Ravens pass in the Steelers end zone to clinch an incredible win.

As the stadium erupted and the party began, Journeyman thanked the Pittsburgh faithful saying; "This win is for this great city, these great fans, and all of Steeler Country! Thank you so much for giving me the chance to call this place home!"

You're welcome, Joe. And THANK YOU for the fireworks!

rest of the **NFL** in **VOLUME 2** . . . .

The Making of Joe Journeyman...

- Jed and David were childhood friends who drifted apart at the end of 9th grade.

- After 13 years, they reconnected by chance at a local hangout. Jed was unemployed, struggling to find work, and expecting his first child.

- Jed decided to show David his portfolio out of the trunk of his car.

- Through all of the adversity, Jed never stopped creating art, always searching for an opportunity to do what he was born to do.

- Unbeknownst to Jed, David operated a consumer products business called IDNA Brands.

- After looking at Jed's portfolio, David offered Jed a job without knowing what Jed would be doing on Monday morning.

- For the next 6 months, Jed completed random projects, including building his own studio (literally), as David obsessed about what to have Jed do next.

- Then, on March 2nd, 2012, David had the idea for Joe Journeyman.

- After thousands of ideas, and countless brainstorming sessions, Jed continues to use his God-given ability to do what he loves to do – create art and inspire those who are still searching for that one opportunity to pursue their dream.

Jed Bruce, Artist   David Bazzoni, Author

"Joe Journeyman changed my life...
I hope in some crazy way he changes yours, too.
Great things will happen if you just don't quit."

Always Keep Searching!

Jed Z Bru

NEW ENGLAND PATRIOTS

- School of Fish
- Lobster Rolls
- Alligator Selfie
- Four Wheel Drive
- Artistic Woodpeckers
- Cow Tipping
- Flag Football
- Headlight Lantern
- Periscope
- Toucan
- BEARly Victorious
- Olive Sword Fight
- Lobster Hot Tub
- Suction Cup High Five
- Grilled Bones
- Sun Tanning Clams
- Wax Tail Surprise
- Tea Party
- New England Chalk Art
- Horseshoe Service
- Wig Thief
- CORNhole Game
- Crab Cake Surprise
- Hippo Photo Bomb

PITTSBURGH STEELERS

- Cheetah Treadmill
- Spirited Mummy
- Horned Biker Club
- Angry Ravens
- Hooved DJ
- Rhino Ring Toss
- Sun Roof Driver
- Sinking Hippo
- Water Slide
- Hippo Crane Operator
- Grilling Fish
- Crocodile Coxswain
- Shielded Soldier
- Balancing Traffic Act
- Hot Dog Contest
- Lemurs x 2
- Hamburger Tower
- Ostrich
- Ear Flop Blindfold
- Hard Hat Wearing Bird
- Kangaroo Double Take
- Mr. and Mrs. Bee
- Canine Hand Car
- Tangled Camera Cord

GREEN BAY PACKERS

- Two Miners
- Skunk Curling
- Snow Owl
- 2 Pigs on a Chopper
- "GO PACK" Ice Sculpture
- Polar Bear Dip
- Snoozing Bear
- Bobsled Course
- Buck in Hot Water
- Dunk Tank
- Wedding Ceremony
- Tangled Paratrooper
- Grizzly Bear Snowball
- Hot Rod Cheese Car
- Hot Headed Walrus
- Bathtub Snowmobile
- Igloo
- Snowman Building a Snowman
- Diver who missed the mark
- Giraffe
- Snow Plowing Rhino
- Odd Pair Ice Fishing
- Headless Snowmobiler
- A Bear in a Pinch

MINNESOTA VIKINGS

- Photo Booth
- Tug of War
- Fish out of Water
- ToadSTOOL
- Field Goal Catapult
- Pumpkin Pi
- Shoe Horned Hat
- Underwear Surrender
- Viking Valet
- Big Fish Little Fish
- Texting Tailgate
- Tooth Fairy
- Blowing Bubbles
- Rockin' Chair
- Fly Away Helmet
- Drumstick Drummer
- JAYwalking
- Doggy Paddling
- Pig Chasing Viking
- Viking Pedicure
- Weeping Willow
- Fish in Life Jackets
- Toupee Snag
- Food Court

DALLAS COWBOYS

- Bare Bear
- Crowd Surfer
- Imposter Cheerleader
- Pain in the Rear
- Chameleon
- Prickly Goal Post
- Fiddler
- Rodeo Ostrich
- COWbell
- Monster Truck Weenie Roast
- Field Goal without a Chance
- Texas-sized Sportula
- Oil Rig Rodeo
- Jumbo Boot Race
- Multitasking Octopus
- Peacock Obstruction
- Gobbling Fan
- Falling Hare
- Rowdy Pelican
- Not so Sheepish Sheep
- Family of Skunks
- Fan with many Boots
- Pigskin Bull Ride
- Hump Day Camels

WASHINGTON REDSKINS

- ROWmans
- Fish Fry
- DUCK!
- 2 Gold Tusked Elephants
- Walking Sticks
- Bear Pause
- Grass Hopper
- Quack Sack
- KaYAK
- Shrimp Cocktail
- Hog Wash
- Pork Belly Fans
- Debate
- Blue Crab Blues Band
- CASTING Ballot
- Wide Retriever
- Fish Tank
- Shrimp Skimpy
- M-Peach
- Pooch Punt
- River Bank
- InvestiGATOR
- Swing Vote
- Charley Horse

CHICAGO BEARS

- Runaway Dog
- Birdseye View Tailgate
- Kangaroo in a Pinch
- Rock Star Camels
- Bear Bath
- Fly Away Toupee
- TP Party
- Reporting the News
- BEAR Angler
- Shark Bait
- Sidewalk Saxophone
- GRILLed Cheese
- Lookout Pirate
- Scuba Diver
- Burnt Hot Dog
- Stretching for Land
- Snoozing Ice Fisherman
- Fishy Game of Football
- Sky High Surfer
- Pogo Stick Delivery
- BEAR Hug
- Tongue Tied Worker
- Break Dancing Penguin
- 1985 Time Machine

PHILADELPHIA EAGLES

- Hitchhiking Hare
- Banana Splits
- WOOLY Mammoth
- Pillow Fight
- Hole in One
- Hoots n' Suits
- Skateboarder
- Fire Ants
- BORNreceiver
- Runaway Mouse
- Talon Shine
- Praying Mantis
- FLY Fishing
- Barber Shop
- Proud Parents to be
- Stroller Play Date
- Sewing School
- Eagle Checking the Wind
- Wing Span Measurement
- EGGscape
- Shoe Tying Mishap
- Snoozing Cowboy
- Chef's Choice Heads or Tails
- Bird Bath

JOE

TED

POLLY

LEON